# LAUGH IT UP, STARE IT DOWN

### Alan Hruska

I0139484

**BROADWAY PLAY PUBLISHING INC**
New York
www.broadwayplaypublishing.com
info@broadwayplaypublishing.com

Cover artwork: Kurt Firla Design & Animation

I S B N: 978-0-88145-654-7

First printing: January 2016

Book design: Marie Donovan
Page make-up: Adobe Indesign
Typeface: Palatino
Printed and bound in the U S A

LAUGHT IT UP, STARE IT DOWN was first produced at the Cherry Lane Theatre, opening on 9 September 2015. The cast and creative contributors were:

JOE.................................................................Jayce Bartok
CLEO.........................................................Katya Campbell
DR MALONE/STEPHEN/CHALMERS/
ARTURO.....................................................Maury Ginsberg
WAITRESS/NURSE LEAVING/DOROTHY/
ALBERTA................................................. Amy Hargreaves

Director...................................................Chris Eigeman
Scenic design.............................................Kevin Judge
Costume design.......................................Jennifer Caprio
Lighting design....................................... Matthew J Fick
Original music & sound design.........................Peter Salett

# CHARACTERS

JOE, *a graduate student of liberal arts who becomes an arbitrage wizard*
CLEO, *an anthropologist*
WAITRESS, *a server at a small French restaurant*
DR MALONE, *a physician who delivers* CLEO's *and* JOE's *child*
NURSE LEAVING, *a nurse who works for* DR MALONE
STEPHEN, *an astrophysicist*
DOROTHY, *a biologist*
CHALMERS, *a burglar*
ALBERTA, *a neighbor to* JOE *and* CLEO
ARTURO, *a tour guide in Venice*

*(All male roles other than* JOE *are played by a single actor, as are all female roles other than* CLEO.*)*

# ACT ONE

## Scene 1

*(Lights up on* JOE, *a young man wearing a blazer, slacks and a striped shirt open at the collar. He stands on a street corner next to a bench, deep in thought.)*

*(Upstage, in the half darkness: a narrow bed, a sink and a stove [convertible to a bar], a small round table with two wooden chairs, a well-designed sofa and two upholstered chairs, a queen-sized bed, and night stands with a lamp on each.)*

*(Above it all, just barely in view, is a large and elaborate red chandelier.)*

*(Enter* CLEO, *a young woman: her eyeglasses and general attire make her look bookish, and in fact she carries a scholarly tome. Taking one look at* JOE, *she's about to walk off, when—)*

JOE: Hold on for the moment, would you?

CLEO: Are you talking to me?

*(*JOE *looks around, pretending to be searching for other people.)*

JOE: I am.

CLEO: *(Impatiently)* Well?

JOE: You're in a hurry?

CLEO: As you can see.

JOE: The thing is, I was standing here.

CLEO: Yes, I gathered that.

JOE: And if you continue, as you're doing—rushing down the street—well *then!*

*(Beat)*

CLEO: What exactly is it that you want?

JOE: I don't necessarily *want anything.* I'm simply commenting on a fact that might otherwise have escaped your attention.

CLEO: About you?

JOE: About the both of us. About the consequences to us both, if you leave.

(CLEO *scrutinizes* JOE *from head to foot.)*

CLEO: *(Warming up for a put-down)* I see. This—this moment you've asked me to hold on for—is a crossroads in our lives.

JOE: You say it lightly.

CLEO: Well, that's not right, is it? One should be more respectful of crossroads.

JOE: Some…crossroads.

CLEO: Like this one. So filled with potential.

JOE: It is, actually.

CLEO: *(Making a mockery of it)* No doubt! Just think. We might go for a coffee, then off for dinner, a violent affair, marriage, babies, houses, trips, celebrations, diseases and funerals. *(Changing tone)* Or I might walk away and never see you again, or think about you for as much as a second.

JOE: If you can imagine all that….

CLEO: *(Scoffing)* Why not go for the coffee?

JOE: Exactly.

CLEO: The thing is, young man.

JOE: Joe.

CLEO: The thing is, Joe, I've already had my crossroads. His name is George. And I'm running late on meeting him right now. So, while I don't like to be rude, even to loiterers who accost me on street corners—

JOE: Big mistake.

CLEO: I beg your pardon?

JOE: Off to see George, is that your plan? *(He clucks at this disparagingly.)* Fool's errand.

CLEO: What?!

JOE: You have no true feelings for George.

CLEO: You're saying this based on the long duration of our acquaintance.

JOE: There's really no need to settle.

CLEO: Settle?!

JOE: On anything less than ecstatic love.

CLEO: *(Incredulous)* Which is how I'd feel about you, you're suggesting, if only I'd join you for a coffee.

JOE: In time, maybe. Whereas with George—

CLEO: You obviously know nothing whatever about George!

JOE: I do know this. He is not—poor fellow—someone capable of inspiring ecstatic love. At least in you. In someone with less imagination or creativity, maybe. But not in you.

CLEO: So you do this often?

JOE: I was waiting for you.

CLEO: *(Triumphantly)* What I thought!

JOE: No, no. I didn't mean waiting here, now. I meant waiting…. *(A bit of awkward pausing, until he breaks forth.)* Well then! Let me properly introduce myself. My full name is Joseph P Allworthy.

CLEO: *(A bit softer in tone)* You've made that up.

JOE: I'm afraid not. But—I'm sure you'll have no trouble believing *this*—the name is not as Trollopean as might appear.

CLEO: He reads Trollope!

JOE: I do.

CLEO: But is not in fact worthy.

JOE: Well, not *all*…worthy. The fact is, I seem to have the total variety of human traits—good and bad.

CLEO: In which case, your name's in *no sense* Trollopean.

JOE: Oh?

CLEO: Not only are you yourself only *partially* worthy, at best; the name comes from Fielding, not Trollope.

JOE: Right. Are these authors George is fond of?

CLEO: Don't you dare belittle George!

JOE: I'd never!

CLEO: *(Sharply)* He is totally off-limits.

*(JOE raises his hands as if to indicate the subject is closed.)*

CLEO: And I'll tell you what's sad.

JOE: Please.

CLEO: *(Ridiculing)* Romantic love?!

JOE: There's a lot of very successful writing on the subject.

CLEO: Well, there would be, wouldn't there. It's exactly the sort of drivel that sells. But there are other kinds of books.

JOE: The ones that don't sell.

CLEO: Not widely. They wouldn't sell widely. Because they remind people of an unpleasant truth.

JOE: That romantic love doesn't last, you're saying.

CLEO: It doesn't exist! People are messy. They're complicated. They're inconsistent, incoherent, and neurotic. They don't live up. Certainly not to a romantic ideal. All you need is a bit of intimacy to kill the illusion.

JOE: Wow. *(Joking)* What are you? An anthropologist?

CLEO: Yes.

*(A double take by JOE.)*

JOE: No, I mean, seriously, what do you do?

CLEO: Anthropology. That's what I do. As seriously as I can.

JOE: And where do you do it?

CLEO: At the university of course. There's very little call for anthropologists at, say, General Motors. *(Beat)* Need, I suppose, but not call.

JOE: I've studied anthropology. Sociology and psychology too. In fact, I've studied most everything.

CLEO: In a dilettantish sort of way.

JOE: Admittedly. But my point, which I think *you've* missed—I wasn't talking about mere romantic love. I referred to ecstatic love, which is a much larger proposition.

CLEO: Even more illusory.

*(Beat)*

JOE: Let's continue this over a cup of coffee.

CLEO: Where you would hope to convince me?

JOE: Where I would hope to seduce you.

CLEO: With one cup of coffee?

JOE: You've already said where that would lead.

CLEO: With the same probability as my being reincarnated as a radish.

(CLEO *darts forward, and* JOE *stands aside to let her pass.*

JOE: It doesn't matter.

*(This surprises* CLEO, *and she hesitates.)*

JOE: Go or stay—I know exactly how this will turn out…Cleo.

CLEO: You know my name.

JOE: Yes.

CLEO: I knew yours too, Joe.

*(Lights fade, but not to black—then up to:)*

## Scene Two

*(*JOE's *room—two weeks later.)*

*(Upstage, with the simple bed, stove and sink. On the wall are reproductions of Egon Schiele drawings.)*

*(The large red chandelier is now slightly lower.)*

*(Enter* CLEO *and* JOE. *He's wearing the same clothes, without the jacket; she's in a blue tee shirt and wrap-around denim skirt.)*

CLEO: *(Taken aback) This* is your apartment?

JOE: Yes.

CLEO: It's only one room!

JOE: I'm only one person.

CLEO: *(Pointing to a door)* A single closet?

JOE: That's the bathroom

CLEO: Where's the closet?

JOE: Under the bed. It's actually a trunk.

CLEO: Where do you hang your things?

JOE: I've just the one jacket. Which I hang on the shower bar.

CLEO: Where do you put it when you're taking a shower?

JOE: I put it on the bed.

*(Beat)*

CLEO: Do you realize how pathetic this is?

JOE: It's all how you think about it.

CLEO: How *do* you think about it, Joe?

JOE: I try not to, actually.

CLEO: Have you no money at all?

JOE: I'm not wanting.

CLEO: No interest, you're saying, in material things.

JOE: Oh, I'm interested.

CLEO: Not enough, however. To earn the cash to buy them.

JOE: Not until now.

*(Silence)*

CLEO: Harumph. *(She inspects the room more closely.)* You read a great deal, but you have no books.

JOE: True.

CLEO: Books do furnish a room.

JOE: And clutter it.

CLEO: You're against clutter.

JOE: I prefer...what you see.

CLEO: Egon Schiele.

JOE: Stirs the soul, don't you think?

CLEO: If it's tortured. Is yours, Joe?

JOE: I wouldn't have thought so, no.

CLEO: How *would* you describe yourself?

JOE: To whom?

CLEO: To me, Joe! I'm the one standing here.

JOE: I'd say...I'm a person of considerable patience.

Beat.

CLEO: Is that a pointed remark?

JOE: Does it feel pointed?

CLEO: It feels barbed.

JOE: Only directed.

CLEO: To me!

JOE: You *are* the one standing there.

*(Silence)*

CLEO: It's been only two weeks we've been seeing each other.

JOE: Every day of.

CLEO: One must get to know one.

JOE: And do you feel you have?

CLEO: *(Looking over the room)* Well, I had thought so.

JOE: It's the place, you're saying.

CLEO: Illegal immigrants live in better apartments.

JOE: Yes, but there are usually more of them per room. Would you like some tea?

CLEO: You have tea?

JOE: Or sherry, if you prefer.

CLEO: Tea and sherry, my, my.

JOE: The essential food groups, yes.

(CLEO *looks around again.*)

CLEO: There's no place to sit.

JOE: There's the bed.

(CLEO *looks at it, then at* JOE, *then back to the bed, frowns and sits on the edge of it.*)

CLEO: Tea would be lovely.

JOE: Coming up. (*He goes to the sink, fills up a kettle, plunks it on a two-burner stove.*)

CLEO: Joe?

(*Sitting alongside* CLEO:)

JOE: Yes?

CLEO: Will you always want to live in a place like this?

JOE: You mean, if we were to live together, would I insist on housing you in a hovel?

CLEO: Would you?

JOE: (*With a flourish*) We can live wherever you want.

CLEO: Could you afford something a trifle more… livable?

JOE: Not at the moment.

CLEO: But you said you'll try?

JOE: Cleo! You're planning our future, and we haven't even made love yet?

CLEO: We will!

(JOE *gives* CLEO *a questioning look.*)

CLEO: I'm an anthropologist, Joe! I know what's expected!

JOE: But not anticipated by you with any enthusiasm?

CLEO: I'm a bit nervous, that's all.

JOE: You're not going to tell me you're a virgin?

CLEO: Of course not.

JOE: Something close, though.

CLEO: I've had two very…unfulfilling experiences.

JOE: Ours might be different. We *are* drawn to each other. We wouldn't be here, if we weren't.

CLEO: Well, *I* wouldn't be.

JOE: You're suggesting what? *I'm* in it only for the unbridled sex?

CLEO: Probably.

(JOE *laughs.*)

JOE: I think we should start by taking our clothes off.

CLEO: See, that's always the problem.

JOE: You're embarrassed?

CLEO: Having someone look at you naked for the first time? Oh no. Why should that matter to me?

JOE: Do you know what year this is?

CLEO: You think I'm old-fashioned.

JOE: (*Groucho-esque*) I think you're delightful. Take off your clothes.

(*Tense silence*)

JOE: We'll turn the lights off.

CLEO: No!

(*Whistling sound*)

CLEO: Isn't that the….

JOE: *(Resigned)* Right.

(JOE *goes to make the tea. While he's at it:)*

CLEO: Joe?

JOE: Yes, darling?

CLEO: Shouldn't we take this in more…graceful stages?

JOE: Having sex, you mean?

CLEO: Yes. We've had lovely days, finding each other, and now I've come to your apartment, such as it is….

(JOE *delivers the tea.)*

JOE: So then you drink your tea and go home?

CLEO: No, I'll stay awhile. We can lie down together.

JOE: After removing our clothes?

CLEO: There you go again.

JOE: Some of our clothes?

CLEO: Very few.

JOE: Is this a negotiation?

CLEO: No, Joe!

JOE: Tell you what. We take off all our clothes, but then just hold each other.

CLEO: *All*…our clothes?

JOE: We can keep our underwear on.

CLEO: Wouldn't that be…frustrating?

*(Beat)*

JOE: As compared to what?

CLEO: You could endure it?

JOE: I could.

CLEO: Are you sure?

JOE: Cleo!

CLEO: Done!

JOE: Deal. *(He puts his tea on the floor and starts unbuttoning his shirt.)*

CLEO: Do you have any biscuits?

JOE: I do.

CLEO: Love one.

*(JOE laughs ruefully, goes for the biscuits, brings CLEO the box. She takes one and starts nibbling. He watches, still standing.)*

CLEO: *(Demurely)* None for you?

JOE: Cleo, why are you being so skittish? Sex can really be fun. Billions of people seem to enjoy it.

CLEO: It's the positions.

JOE: Well, there are some less undignified than others.

CLEO: There are none…that are dignified.

JOE: As an anthropologist, you may have over-studied the subject.

CLEO: Maybe. But I can't help what I think.

JOE: Y'know what I think?

CLEO: What?

JOE: You ought to stop thinking.

CLEO: Just mindless sex.

JOE: The best kind.

*(CLEO frowns.)*

JOE: Cleo, come here.

*(After a moment's reflection, CLEO does what's asked.)*

*(JOE drapes his arms on her shoulders.)*

JOE: You're still very young—in heart and mind—I understand that, but—

CLEO: You mean stop acting like a schoolgirl.

JOE: No. Today's schoolgirl would be far more advanced.

CLEO: I am sorry. Is this really driving you crazy?

JOE: It would, if I hadn't already made the journey.

CLEO: You said you knew how we'd turn out.

JOE: It's the pace I hadn't quite anticipated.

CLEO: I'm pretty slow.

JOE: Glaciers are known to move faster.

CLEO: I'm not a glacier, Joe. I'm not cold.

(JOE *looks at* CLEO *skeptically.*)

CLEO: I feel desire for you.

JOE: Do you?

CLEO: Of course. I'm burning with it.

JOE: Then there's no problem.

CLEO: Ha! It's not you with your legs in the air, or bent over on all fours—

JOE: It could be.

(CLEO *laughs.*)

CLEO: I want to sleep with you. I just want to get there...gradually. (*She moves to one side and unbuttons her blouse.*)

JOE: Gradually, yes.

CLEO: I don't want to rush things.

JOE: You do what you're comfortable doing. (*He quickly unbuttons his own shirt and removes it, standing completely bare to the waist.*)

CLEO: I can't do that...now.

(CLEO *removes her blouse and skirt.* JOE *goes to her and holds her.*)

JOE: Are you okay?

CLEO: Yes, Joe.

JOE: Not in shock?

CLEO: No, Joe.

JOE: Should we lie down now?

CLEO: Just hold me like this.

JOE: Okay.

(*After a few moments,* JOE's *hand meanders down* CLEO's *back to squeeze her bottom.*)

CLEO: No fair!

JOE: Why's that?

CLEO: It's designed to make me want to have sex.

(JOE *backs off.*)

JOE: Absolutely true. Carefully crafted, time-tested, focus-grouped through the ages. Almost never fails to work.

CLEO: You're making fun of me.

JOE: We are—the both of us—fairly comical at this moment.

CLEO: All right then.

JOE: (*Surprised, but still wary*) All right?

CLEO: We can lie down on the bed, and you can touch me all over, until I get so aroused I'll do anything.

JOE: Wow.

CLEO: So?

JOE: You know this about yourself?

CLEO: Of course I do.

JOE: And you want it?

CLEO: Of course I want it.

JOE: Then what really has been the problem?

CLEO: Oh Joe!

JOE: What?

CLEO: I wanted so much for us to be different.

*(Lights fade—then up to:)*

## Scene 3

*(CLEO and JOE sit at the small round table with two chairs: a cozy French restaurant.)*

*(The large red chandelier is now a bit lower.)*

JOE: Service is exceptionally slow at this place.

CLEO: It is.

JOE: Which may explain why all the tables are empty.

CLEO: It may.

JOE: Have you seen a waitress?

CLEO: I'm pregnant.

*(JOE sits back, does a double take.)*

CLEO: It's been building up.

JOE: The pregnancy?!

CLEO: The need to tell you. That I'm pregnant.

JOE: I don't see how it's possible you're pregnant.

CLEO: *(Wryly)* Immaculate conception?

JOE: No, but we *have* been careful.

CLEO: Does it matter how it happened, Joe?

JOE: *(Thinking)* It might.

CLEO: The question is—

JOE: I know the question.

CLEO: *(Sing-song)* And the answer is? *(Hand stretched behind her)* Envelope please!

JOE: The answer is we do the normal happy responsible thing one does when one conceives a child.

CLEO: Have an abortion?

JOE: Is that what you want?

CLEO: You tell me!

JOE: In the twenty or so seconds I've had to consider it?

CLEO: Exactly. Instinctively. What do you want?

JOE: I think we should have the child. I will choose a profession, exert myself devotedly to it, earn immense sums, buy us a house, and we and our children shall live happily ever after.

*(Silence)*

CLEO: Is there any part of that speech that you mean?

JOE: Absolutely all of it. *(Beat. Sincerely)* Really.

CLEO: You take my breath away.

JOE: Mine too.

CLEO: Does marriage figure into any of this?

JOE: That's an optional bit.

CLEO: Whose option?

JOE: Yours of course, darling.

CLEO: You're indifferent?

JOE: Only to the ceremony. Not to the commitment.

CLEO: You consider yourself committed?

JOE: From the moment I saw you. *(Silence)* But there's a question pending. Do *you* want our child?

*(Beat)*

*(CLEO hesitantly nods.)*

JOE: So there's no problem.

CLEO: I spoke of no problem.

JOE: It was in your inflection.

CLEO: My what?

JOE: I said—

CLEO: There might be a problem in there being no problem.

JOE: We need drama?

*(CLEO seems suddenly upset.)*

CLEO: What we need is…a waitress! *(Rising tones)* Is this really a restaurant?!

*(CLEO and JOE look around rather desperately.)*

*(WAITRESS enters with her order pad. She's an attractive woman, a bit past her prime, hair piled high but disheveled, uniform overwhelmed by plaid sweater and bangles.)*

WAITRESS: Do you know what you want?

JOE: We haven't a menu.

WAITRESS: *(Flabbergasted)* No one's given you a menu?!

*(CLEO and JOE both spread their hands to give her a clear view of the table.)*

WAITRESS: I'll be!

*(The WAITRESS leaves. CLEO and JOE look at each other with dubiety.)*

CLEO: I have a very strange feeling about this place.

JOE: We've been here before.

CLEO: I've never seen that waitress before.

JOE: Turnover.

CLEO: *(Fanny Brice)* You want me to turn over?!

JOE: No, I'm simply explaining there's a big turnover in these waitressing jobs.

*(WAITRESS returns with menus, hands one to each.)*

WAITRESS: I'll give you a moment.

*(WAITRESS exits. CLEO and JOE open the menus, begin to turn the pages, then turn them faster to the end.)*

JOE: It's blank.

CLEO: Mine too!

*(JOE rises.)*

JOE: Waitress!

*(WAITRESS returns.)*

WAITRESS: You ready to order?

JOE: *(Sitting with a show of annoyance)* You gave us blank menus.

WAITRESS: Oh my. *(She grabs one and inspects.)* You got the blank ones. Sorry about that. Why don't I just tell you what we have tonight.

JOE: *(Impatiently)* All right.

WAITRESS: Filet of sole.

*(CLEO and JOE wait.)*

JOE: Yes, and?

WAITRESS: It's very good.

CLEO: That's all you have?

WAITRESS: No, but everything else is frozen—has to be defrosted and microwaved. The filet of sole is fresh.

JOE: I thought this was a French restaurant.

WAITRESS: *Certainement!* It is!

CLEO: Do you have starters?

WAITRESS: Of course. Oysters?

JOE: Are they fresh?

*(WAITRESS flips her hand and makes a humming sound, as if to say, "I wouldn't bet on it".)*

CLEO: *(To JOE)* Should we leave?

JOE: *(To the waitress)* Do you have any soup?

WAITRESS: *Naturellement.* Pistou.

*(JOE looks at CLEO, who nods.)*

JOE: We'll have that.

WAITRESS: With the sole?

*(Another nod from CLEO.)*

JOE: Well, before it. And does the sole come with anything?

WAITRESS: There's quite a lot of it.

CLEO: No vegetables?

WAITRESS: You want vegetables?

JOE: It's not an unreasonable request.

WAITRESS: *(Combatively)* You're having vegetable soup.

CLEO: So you think it *is* unreasonable?

WAITRESS: What kind of vegetables would you like?

JOE: Well, what do you have?

WAITRESS: On hand? Right now?

JOE: You have none at all?

WAITRESS: The market's right across the street. I could go there while the chef is defrosting your soup.

JOE: This is ridiculous! Are you actually serving food here?

WAITRESS: Occasionally.

JOE: This doesn't seem to be one of the occasions.

WAITRESS: I know. It's a lottery.

CLEO: We'd prefer a restaurant.

WAITRESS: We do our best. And by the time you might travel to another restaurant, sit down, study a menu, order—the whole process—we would have given you your sole.

JOE: And pistou?

WAITRESS: *(Unconvincingly)* Of course.

*(Beat)*

CLEO: She has a point.

JOE: Put a rush on it.

WAITRESS: *(Archly formal) Naturellement. (She exits.)*

CLEO: What's happened to this place?

JOE: It's the natural order of things.

CLEO: Entropy.

JOE: I'm afraid so.

CLEO: Not us.

JOE: Not us.

CLEO: You spoke of immense sums.

JOE: Ah. That got your attention.

CLEO: It did. Having raised the question of how you might amass them.

JOE: It can't be that hard. Thousands of stunted, grasping, narrow-minded trolls seem to do it all the time.

CLEO: That may be the secret.

JOE: Narrow mindedness? Total focus on that goal?

CLEO: Don't you think?

JOE: Perhaps there's an exception.

CLEO: Oh, I do hope you're good at it, Joe, because I'm not.

*(Beat)*

JOE: You sound worried.

CLEO: Of course I'm worried.

JOE: About?

CLEO: You think there's nothing to be worried about?

JOE: Well, in a general sort of way.

CLEO: There are vicissitudes.

JOE: Anything specific?

CLEO: Everything. Is. Specific.

JOE: You're worried about losing your job?

CLEO: Every day.

JOE: Your health?

CLEO: Certainly.

JOE: Earthquakes?

CLEO: They're very common here.

JOE: Hurricanes and tidal surges?

CLEO: I told you, Joe! Everything! *There is a potential for disaster in everything!* And we're about to produce a child into this…this maelstrom of uncertainty, this --

*(WAITRESS enters with two very small bowls on a tray.)*

WAITRESS: Pistou!

*(Lights fade—then up to:)*

## Scene 4

*(The single bed, now isolated, a single chair alongside it—a hospital room.)*

*(The large red chandelier is just a trifle lower.)*

*(CLEO is in bed. JOE arrives, kisses her, seats himself on the chair.)*

JOE: Little Harry is good?

CLEO: Yes, he is.

JOE: You're good?

CLEO: Yes, I am.

JOE: We're still on schedule?

CLEO: That we are. Being released tomorrow, first thing.

JOE: Excellent.

*(Beat)*

CLEO: And your currency transaction?

JOE: *(As if trying to recall)* Oh, yes?

CLEO: *(As if reminding him)* Rupees?

JOE: We did the rupees.

CLEO: *(Getting excited)* Made a fortune, didn't we!

JOE: Did all right, yes.

CLEO: *(Getting impatient)* How all right, Joe?

JOE: A million and a half all right, give or take.

CLEO: Inspired, darling! Rupees!

JOE: It's where the dart hit the wall. At least the algorithmic equivalent.

CLEO: Had it come up shekels—

JOE: Bellies up for us!

CLEO: *(Enthusiastically)* Chum for the sea gulls.

*(Beat)*

JOE: A bit florid that, but yes.

*(Enter DR MALONE, an urbanely handsome man about ten years older than JOE. The stark authority of his buttoned-up white coat is softened by a practiced smile. He holds a file in one hand.)*

DR MALONE: Ah. The both of you. How good.

JOE: Doctor, thank you for stopping by.

DR MALONE: Not at all. Not at all. Particular reason, actually.

JOE: To see the patient.

DR MALONE: Yes, of course.

JOE: Well, here she is.

DR MALONE: *(Brightly)* Yes, yes. *(Change of tone)* There was another reason.

JOE: Oh?

DR MALONE: You're in currencies, as I recall.

JOE: In and out, as it were.

DR MALONE: Exactly. Nerves of steel, eh? Used to shocks, are you?

JOE: *(Suspiciously)* One tries to limit those.

DR MALONE: A man of your expertise.

JOE: There's little of that going around. Currency swings—up, down; black, red; totally unpredictable. Not much better than roulette.

DR MALONE: Where the house is likely tipping the wheel.

JOE: Lots of people are tipping the currency, but they're tipping it up or down, not to a house number.

DR MALONE: We sometimes have that situation here, don't you know.

JOE: Tipping the wheel? In medicine?

DR MALONE: *(Flatly)* In hospitals.

*(Beat)*

CLEO: *(Coldly)* Are you trying to tell us something, Doctor?

DR MALONE: I am.

*(CLEO and JOE stare at him.)*

DR MALONE: Something a bit difficult to say.

CLEO: I think you'd better just say it.

DR MALONE: *(Cheerfully)* We seem—hopefully only for the moment—to have misplaced... *(Consulting the file)* ...Harry, was it?

CLEO: *(Incipient panic)* You've lost our baby?!

DR MALONE: Only for the moment. I'm sure we'll find him... *(Shakily)* soon.

JOE: That's what you came by to tell us?!

DR MALONE: Not exactly. I came by to make sure he wasn't in here.

CLEO: *(Panic)* You've absolutely no idea where he is?

DR MALONE: There are only a limited number of possibilities.

CLEO: *(Screaming)* Like someone kidnapped him!

DR MALONE: Well, yes, that would be one of the possibilities.

*(CLEO screams even louder.)*

DR MALONE: Please, Mrs Allworthy.

CLEO: Get out of here and find my baby!

DR MALONE: Absolutely.

(CLEO *rises from bed.*)

CLEO: I'm going too.

JOE: You stay, I'll go.

(*Enter* NURSE LEAVING, *who looks remarkably like the waitress in the earlier scene [and, in fact is played by the same actor].*)

NURSE LEAVING: Doctor!

DR MALONE: Ah, Nurse Leaving.

NURSE LEAVING: May I speak to you privately, Doctor?

DR MALONE: We've found the child?!

NURSE LEAVING: Oh, they know.

DR MALONE: We've just been discussing it, yes.

NURSE LEAVING: Oh dear, and now everyone's upset. No need. No need at all. Your baby is quite safe, very happy, sleeping peacefully. Totally found.

CLEO: Thank God!

NURSE LEAVING: No scars whatever.

CLEO: No scars?!

NURSE LEAVING: Figure of speech. I mean simply, this little episode, lamentable as it might be, went right over your baby's head. Henry is it?

CLEO & JOE: Harry!

NURSE LEAVING: Harry, yes.

CLEO: What exactly happened, Nurse Leaving?

NURSE LEAVING: (*Soothingly*) He's returned to the nursery. He won't remember anything at all about this.

JOE: Why did he ever *leave* the nursery?

NURSE LEAVING: Technically, he didn't leave the nursery. After leaving here, that is.

CLEO: You mean he never got there.

NURSE LEAVING: Not directly.

CLEO: He left here with you!

NURSE LEAVING: Correct.

CLEO: You left him somewhere on route to the nursery.

NURSE LEAVING: It happens.

JOE: Where did you leave him?!

NURSE LEAVING: Well.

JOE: Yes?!

NURSE LEAVING: In the Ladies.

CLEO: You left my boy in the ladies room?

NURSE LEAVING: He's only a little boy.

JOE: For how long?!

NURSE LEAVING: Couldn't have been that long.

DR MALONE: Nurse, I think we should discuss this in my office.

JOE: I don't think so. Not until we have the full story. Indeed, not until I've seen my son. You're sure it is my son.

NURSE LEAVING: Oh yes. I read his tag. Henry.

CLEO & JOE: *Henry?!*

NURSE LEAVING: I mean, Harry.

CLEO: *(Wailing)* How could you have done this?!

NURSE LEAVING: Honest answer?

JOE: *(Sarcastically)* Preferably.

NURSE LEAVING: *(Shrugging)* I had to pee.

JOE: My God! And you couldn't have brought him to the nursery first?

NURSE LEAVING: I had to pee real bad.

JOE: And then, coming out of the stall, you walked right by him?!

NURSE LEAVING: I'm afraid, by that point…my mind was elsewhere.

JOE: Doctor Malone!

DR MALONE: All's well that ends well, wouldn't you say?

NURSE LEAVING: *(With a bright smile)* I would! *(She makes a fluttering, smiling exit.)*

JOE: I wouldn't. No. Not in these circumstances. You are, I believe the head of this hospital.

DR MALONE: It's a title.

JOE: Surely some action by the hospital is indicated!

DR MALONE: Absolutely. We will do everything humanly possible to ensure nothing like this can ever happen again.

JOE: That's it?!

DR MALONE: *(Upbeat)* That's it.

JOE: And will that involve doing anything more than you're now doing?

DR MALONE: Frankly?

*(JOE looks at DR MALONE contemptuously.)*

DR MALONE: No.

CLEO: That's pathetic!

DR MALONE: *(Emphatically)* I agree. Would you like me to fire Nurse Leaving?

JOE: You'd do that?

DR MALONE: Oh yes.

CLEO: And hire someone more competent?

DR MALONE: That's not likely.

JOE: Any nurse you can hire is capable of leaving babies in the ladies room?

DR MALONE: Or worse.

JOE: *Worse?!*

DR MALONE: Far worse.

JOE: You've no way of screening out the most egregious cases?

DR MALONE: Oh, the most egregious—you've no idea. Yes, we can weed *those* out.

JOE: And beyond that?

DR MALONE: Like throwing darts at a wall. *(With a flamboyant gesture, he exits.)*

*(CLEO and JOE look at each other as if comparing notes on the absurdity of what they'd just witnessed.)*

CLEO: Are they bringing our baby?

JOE: I assume so.

CLEO: *(Irritably)* Did they say?

JOE: *(Guiltily acknowledging he left the question open)* I'll go check.

CLEO: What kind of people are these?!

JOE: They did deliver the child.

CLEO: Cavemen could deliver a child!

JOE: True.

*(Beat)*

CLEO: You're being rather tolerant.

JOE: Accidents do happen.

CLEO: You mean disasters!

JOE: Yes.

CLEO: Which can always strike.

JOE: At any moment.

CLEO: Acts of friends.

JOE: Acts of strangers.

CLEO: Acts of God.

JOE: The biggest stranger.

*(Silence)*

CLEO: *(Wailing)* Get our child, Joe! Let's get out of here!

*(Lights fade.)*

END OF ACT ONE

*(—then up to:)*

# ACT TWO

## Scene 1

*(Five years later)*

*(Night)*

*(The designer sofa and upholstered chairs—now set in a large modern living room, with windows offering a spectacular view of the stars over the rooftops of the dark city.)*

*(And again—)*

*(The large red chandelier is marginally lower.)*

*(CLEO and JOE entertain friends: STEPHEN, an astrophysicist [same actor who played DR MALONE], and his wife, DOROTHY, a professor of biology at the university [same actor who played the WAITRESS and NURSE]. STEPHEN is a dogmatist, given to pomposity, and DOROTHY, a long sufferer of these traits.)*

*(The four, assembled on the sofa and chairs, rise separately from time to time to pour drinks at the bar.)*

STEPHEN: Something went very wrong there.

JOE: Where? What?

STEPHEN: This friend of mine—young guy—ran a hedge fund even bigger than yours—

JOE: I just work there.

STEPHEN: Work there?! Just fucking work there?! Like a fucking rock star! A fucking guru.

JOE: Easy, Stephen.

STEPHEN: Open the papers, turn on the tube—it's Joe Allworthy. On the yuan. The euro. The dong.

JOE: You know about the dong?

STEPHEN: Who doesn't know about the fucking dong?

DOROTHY: *(Caustically)* Rhymes with thong.

*(Beat)*

CLEO: Why even say that?

DOROTHY: *(Shrugging, as if obvious)* Dong, thong?

JOE: *(Joking)* Not an association *Stephen* would make. *His* mind being on the heavens.

DOROTHY: *(Sardonically)* Oh, really?

*(Silence)*

JOE: This friend of yours, Stephen? The one with the hedge fund....

STEPHEN: As I said, he died.

JOE: Died? No, you hadn't said.

STEPHEN: Well, he did. Here one day; ash the next. Just...*poof!*

JOE: Jesus. How old was he?

STEPHEN: Our age. Cuts himself. Damn thing gets infected. So what would you think? Half a billion net worth—pretty likely he'd find someone with *something* to help, right? A little dab'll do ya? A little needle in the tushy? Something theraputic, for crissake! But no! Fifty fucking doctors stand there watching sepsis bloom. *(Sing-song)* See how all the organs fail. Kaput! Bye, bye! Gone.

CLEO: Well, that's an awful story.

STEPHEN: I keep telling you guys! In my profession, I live with far more awful stories than this.

JOE: *(Mocking incredulity)* As an astrophysicist?

STEPHEN: Yes! The point exactly!

CLEO: So, your friend—fate or chance?

STEPHEN: *(With a scoffing laugh)* Fate? You believe in fate?

CLEO: I'm agnostic on the subject.

DOROTHY: Everyone has a fate, dear.

STEPHEN: *(As if performing an introduction)* My wife, your friend—young Dorothea. A biologist and a recovering alcoholic. Interesting combination, don't you think. She studies the genes, the D N A, the R N A, et cetera, et cetera., and comes up with, guess what?

JOE: Most everyone believes in a higher power, Stephen.

STEPHEN: Which they anthropomorphize into someone looking very much like Morgan Freeman. Who hands out fates like Bingo cards at a church fundraiser.

CLEO: And you? After studying the heavens? Whatta you think's up there? Beyond the telescopes? Way beyond. Say billions of billions of light years beyond.

STEPHEN: You don't want to know.

JOE: No one knows.

STEPHEN: Oh, we know, my dears. Some of us do. And some of us have said. But no one's listening. They don't want to hear.

CLEO: I'm listening.

DOROTHY: I'm not!

STEPHEN: See?

JOE: *(Serious)* What's been said? By your lot? That no one's hearing?

STEPHEN: *(Pompously)* What's up there…is…nothing. Unimaginable eons of nothing. It's implacable. It's malignant. And it's evil. Because ultimately it will turn all life into itself.

*(Silence)*

CLEO: *(Making light of it)* How much time would you say we had left?

STEPHEN: It shouldn't affect your immediate plans… unless you were thinking of going to church.

CLEO: Not my thing. I'm an anthropologist, Stephen. I'm interested in what people believe only because they believe it.

STEPHEN: *(Musingly)* Lovely.

CLEO: What?

STEPHEN: An anthropologist who believes only in people. A biologist who believes deeply in God. A physicist who believes in nothing. And an arbitrage wizard who believes in chance. All in the same room.

CLEO: Sounds like a joke. A minister, a priest and—

DOROTHY: *(Interrupting)* It is a joke.

STEPHEN: Big joke. Which no one seems to be getting.

JOE: Does it matter?

STEPHEN: Of course it bloody well matters.

JOE: What about love?

STEPHEN: What about it?

JOE: As an antidote to nothingness.

STEPHEN: Wonderful illusion. By increasing the pleasure of being alive, it diminishes the discomfort of being meaningless.

CLEO: I used to feel that way.

STEPHEN: And now?

CLEO: Loving Joe and making Harry give me hope of purpose.

STEPHEN: *(Mockingly)* Hope, yes, of course.

JOE: *(Pointedly to* STEPHEN*)* Don't you feel that way about Dorothy?

*(*STEPHEN *says nothing.)*

DOROTHY: We should go back to the thong.

CLEO: Whose thong?!

DOROTHY: *I* don't wear one.

*(Everyone turns to* STEPHEN.*)*

STEPHEN: Don't look at me!

JOE: Difficult not to.

DOROTHY: *(To* CLEO*)* I'm told they can't help themselves.

CLEO: They?!

DOROTHY: Men, of course.

CLEO: Not Joe.

DOROTHY: *(Gently teasing him)* Of course Joe.

JOE: *(Over-reacting)* What?!

*(*CLEO *looks back to* DOROTHY, *who looks away.* STEPHEN *misses the exchange, while mixing himself a drink.)*

CLEO: *(Softly)* Good God.

DOROTHY: Interesting entreaty.

CLEO: It's just an expression.

DOROTHY: For what?

CLEO: For ten seconds ago I had a marriage?

DOROTHY: And now?

STEPHEN: *(Returning to his seat)* Nothing? *(Silence. With a flourish)* This reminds me of the game we used to play: rock, paper, scissors, fire? Except now we have: God, man, chance, nothing—and which do you think prevails?

DOROTHY: *(To* STEPHEN*)* I know what *you* think. We should all be atheists, believing in nothing, thinking everything is permitted, because you and your kind can't resist pussy.

STEPHEN: My kind?

DOROTHY: *Man*kind—whose persistent lunge at almost anything female is like the tropism of a plant.

JOE: You may be confusing fantasies with deeds.

DOROTHY: *(With relish)* Treasonable thoughts were once punishable by decapitation.

JOE: Pretty barbaric.

DOROTHY: *(Chortling)* Oh, I don't know.

CLEO: *(Zoning in)* So which is it, Joe? In your case? The thought or the deed?

JOE: I'll admit to the thoughts. One can't be human without having the thoughts.

CLEO: *I* don't.

(JOE *looks at* CLEO *skeptically.*)

STEPHEN: *(Pontificating condescendingly)* There's no moral difference between wanting the deed and doing it. No culpability to either, mind you—but no moral difference. We've been programmed for pleasure. So why…not…just *fucking…have* it?!

CLEO: This goes for Dorothy as well as you?

STEPHEN: Absolutely. Anyone. Why not?

JOE: Impact on others?

STEPHEN: Are you talking about… *(He makes a face of disdain.)* possessiveness? Jealousy? Haven't you been listening? Given the facts of our tiny existence, for any one of us to want another *not* to have pleasure is extremely selfish. Especially when thousands of us are randomly extinguished every minute.

*(Silence)*

CLEO: Are you quite finished, Stephen?

STEPHEN: You find yourself in disagreement?

CLEO: I find myself drowning in bullshit.

JOE: That was mostly bullshit.

CLEO: Mostly?!

JOE: There are elements in what he said—

CLEO: Have you been fucking someone, Joe?

JOE: Are you back on that?

CLEO: Yes!

JOE: Where is this coming from?

CLEO: Are you?

JOE: Can we just—

CLEO: I'd like an answer to my question!

JOE: It's a ridiculous question.

CLEO: Answer it!

JOE: *(Making light of it)* Before witnesses?

CLEO: Yes.

JOE: Look, if we just—

CLEO: *Now!*

JOE: *(Pleadingly)* Cleo—

CLEO: Now, Joe!

JOE: Please!

CLEO: I'll walk out of here, Joe!

JOE: No you won't!

CLEO: Try me!

JOE: Darling.

CLEO: And I won't come back.

JOE: I'm not sleeping with anyone! Okay?!

CLEO: At the moment! I can see that! How 'bout in the last twelve months?

JOE: This is really absurd!

(CLEO *gets up.*)

CLEO: I'm out of here.

JOE: Stop!

CLEO: Bye, Joe. (*She starts walking.*)

JOE: It was Dorothy.

(CLEO *stops, turns, stares at* JOE.)

JOE: (*Big sigh, and he looks at* DOROTHY) It was Dorothy.

(*Long silence in which* DOROTHY *and* JOE *look down, while* STEPHEN *goes from shock to outrage.*)

STEPHEN: (*With hot fury*) You're fucking my wife?! I'll fucking kill you!

(*Lights snap out.*)

(*Lights snap back up.*)

## Scene 2

(*Minutes later—*DOROTHY *and* STEPHEN *have left.*)

(JOE *sits in silence;* CLEO, *agitatedly, clears the room.*)

CLEO: How could you have?

JOE: How could I not have is the question.

CLEO: You pursued her?!

JOE: We met by chance.

CLEO: Then went off to fuck each other.

(JOE *writhes.*)

CLEO: When *was* this...meeting?

JOE: Just before Christmas.

CLEO: Where?

JOE: The jewelry shop next to their building. *(Hopefully as if it might change things)* I was buying your gift! She was tracking Stephen's. We had some chatter—

CLEO: *(Bitingly)* Social intercourse.

JOE: The very term she used!

CLEO: Before suggesting you take the intercourse upstairs.

JOE: That's how it was!

CLEO: *She* suggested?

JOE: You know I wouldn't have.

CLEO: *(Wryly)* Do I? You apparently failed to think of reasons to decline.

JOE: I knew the reasons.

CLEO: But by that time, she'd taken her clothes off.

JOE: How'd you know?

CLEO: My God, Joe! Don't you have any self-control?

JOE: It seemed impolite, then, almost churlish, not to.

CLEO: Not to fuck her?

JOE: Yes.

CLEO: And did you enjoy it?

JOE: It was the oddest few minutes of my life. An out-of-body experience.

CLEO: You were transported with joy.

JOE: Not with joy, no. It was like I were somewhere up on the ceiling looking down on myself. Wondering why I was doing something so stupid.

CLEO: And what did you conclude?

JOE: That I should finish and leave as quickly as possible. Which I did. Not very satisfying from her standpoint, I'm afraid. Nor from mine, for that matter.

CLEO: *(Sarcastically)* What a shame.

JOE: It was stupid because I knew you'd be hurt. And of course I don't love her; I love you. I don't even like her very much.

CLEO: Which you think excuses you?

JOE: Not from stupidity.

CLEO: *(With exasperation)* From anything?!

JOE: *(Resigned)* Actually, I've been expecting....

CLEO: *(Caustically)* What? Reprisals?

*(JOE rises and begins trying to help clear.)*

JOE: I had a dream last night. Truly awful. There was this...authority figure who talked directly to God. Or at least through an angel.

CLEO: Not me!

JOE: You *are* angelic, darling, but unmistakably feminine.

CLEO: I meant the authority figure.

JOE: He was a man. Who looked like my father. He dragged me to the top of a hill, thumped me down on a rock, flashed a very long knife, and said—or rather proclaimed— "Prepare to be sacrificed!"

CLEO: Did he go through with it?

JOE: No. I talked him out of it. These so-called instructions from God, I explained—totally implausible.

CLEO: Hmm.

JOE: You think I should have been sacrificed?

CLEO: I think you should leave.

JOE: Banished? For one indiscretion?

CLEO: Pack a bag, Joe.

JOE: Do you believe in that kind of God? One who metes out punishments and rewards? One who requires appeasement?

CLEO: Sometimes.

JOE: How could you possibly?

CLEO: In the same way I believe in anything.

(JOE *gives a questioning look.*)

CLEO: Conveniently. Like everyone else. To validate what I already think. To justify what I'm going to do anyway.

*(Beat)*

JOE: Like what?

CLEO: Like throwing you out of this house!

*(Lights fade—then up to:)*

## Scene 3

*(CLEO's home)*

*(CLEO stands thinking in the middle of her living room. Almost immediately, the doorbell rings. Opening the door, she finds DOROTHY.)*

DOROTHY: You surprised me.

CLEO: Not nearly as much as you surprised me.

DOROTHY: No, I mean by inviting me to your home.

CLEO: *Inviting* you?

DOROTHY: Well, summoning. I thought you'd never talk to me again.

CLEO: I'm not sure I will.

(CLEO *heads back towards her living room and* DOROTHY, *impliedly being led, follows.*)

(CLEO *settles back on a chair;* DOROTHY *perches on the edge of the sofa.* CLEO *stares at her former friend, as if working out a puzzle.*)

DOROTHY: *(Nervously, to break the silence)* Actually, I thought you might have brought me here to kill me.

CLEO: *(Ignoring the remark)* Why did you sleep with my husband?

DOROTHY: Never liked that expression. *Sleep with.* One rarely does. Unless you're with your own husband. Then you sleep. Then, typically, you can't wait to sleep. But some new guy you've had a bit of a thing for? Sleep's the last thing you want to do.

CLEO: *(Caustically)* And that's how it was with Joe?

DOROTHY: Joe…was completely different. Totally spontaneous. I trapped Joe. *(She laughs.)* He didn't have a chance.

CLEO: Why? Why'd you do it?

DOROTHY: To get back at Stephen, of course. Joe was just…there, within range. And too polite to refuse me. Don't think he liked any part of it, poor man. And he couldn't escape fast enough once the deed was done. No "sleeping with" there, believe me.

CLEO: And, for you, our friendship didn't enter into it?

DOROTHY: *(With a sigh)* Frankly, I had hoped you'd never find out.

CLEO: Really? You think you were being subtle the other night? Dropping hints like H-bombs?

DOROTHY: H-bombs?

CLEO: No one, possibly, could have missed the point. As much as I might have wanted to.

DOROTHY: Yeah, sorry about that.

CLEO: Pretty damn selfish.

DOROTHY: I admit it. Couldn't see beyond my own anger at that philandering son of a bitch.

CLEO: Whom you'll never forgive.

DOROTHY: That bastard? Never! Glad I shot him down.

CLEO: Leaving me without my Joe.

DOROTHY: For which you'll never forgive me.

CLEO: *(With emphasis)* For which I'll never forgive you.

*(Silence, in which DOROTHY sits back.)*

DOROTHY: Oh, shit.

*(CLEO says nothing.)*

DOROTHY: Made a mess, didn't I?

CLEO: You should leave now.

DOROTHY: Cleo! Let's talk it through more.

CLEO: You've told me what I wanted to know. I'd rather you just left now.

DOROTHY: You'll work it out, though, with Joe.

CLEO: Eventually. Probably. Painfully.

DOROTHY: Funny. You can forgive him, but not me.

CLEO: That's right.

DOROTHY: Why *not* me?

CLEO: What Joe and I have is large…and complicated. There's room in there to work this out. In time. What you and I have—or used to—is a relatively small space. With lines. No room for crossing them. With acts of disloyalty. Like poaching one's husband.

DOROTHY: I didn't keep him very long.

CLEO: Y'know, you're very much like Stephen.

DOROTHY: You mean selfish and egotistical? No doubt. Which is why he and I are totally *un*congenial.

CLEO: But you deserve each other.

DOROTHY: Probably right. But Cleo—are you so pure of heart?

CLEO: I wouldn't sleep with your husband.

DOROTHY: *(As if so obvious)* You're not attracted to him.

CLEO: Are you attracted to Joe?

DOROTHY: *(With a shrug)* I'm attracted to Joe. I'm attracted to you.

CLEO: What the hell does that mean?

DOROTHY: Simple enough. You're good looking, I'm attracted to you.

CLEO: *(Shocked)* You're gay? You're making a pass at me?

DOROTHY: Another one of those words. *Gay.* You don't have to be gay to want to have sex with a woman.

CLEO: You do if you *are* a woman!

DOROTHY: See that's all wrong. Were you at an all-girls boarding school?

CLEO: No.

DOROTHY: Bunch of teenage girls—all sexed up with no boys around. Didn't have to be gay for that to work out.

(CLEO *stands.*)

CLEO: I'm not having sex with you, Dorothy.

(DOROTHY *laughs and stands as well.*)

DOROTHY: Of course you're not. Way over *your* line.

CLEO: Then why'd you...raise it?

DOROTHY: As a distraction. And to see if there's even a glimmer of interest. Which there is. *(Beat)* We don't have that much, y'know. Sex is one of the good things.

CLEO: You really *are* just like him. Even in your hypocrisy.

DOROTHY: Right. I know. It's human. We're all self-centered. Self-entitled. Self-justifying.

CLEO: I realize that, Dorothy. But there are degrees.

DOROTHY: You tamp yours down?

CLEO: If I didn't, you'd already be dead.

(Lights fade—then up to:)

## Scene 4

(*French restaurant*)

(STEPHEN *is seated at a table as* JOE *arrives.*)

STEPHEN: *(Bouncing up)* Joe!

JOE: Stephen!

(*The two shake hands,* JOE *a bit cautiously.*)

JOE: I was so glad you called.

STEPHEN: And surprised?

JOE: Somewhat.

STEPHEN: Sit.

(JOE *and* STEPHEN *do.*)

STEPHEN: I had two reasons, actually. *(He looks around.)* Funny, haven't seen a waitress.

JOE: *(With a laugh)* This place? A waitress?

STEPHEN: The service is slow, you mean.

JOE: Slow is a bit of an understatement, but never mind. Your two reasons?

STEPHEN: Right. I don't want you to be worrying about me and Dorothy and what you think you caused. At most you were a catalyst for our break up. And if it hadn't been you, another, in very short order, would have presented itself. Dorothy and I were designed to explode.

JOE: I'm sorry. And more than sorry for what I did. But I appreciate your taking such a broad-minded view of it.

STEPHEN: Not at all.

JOE: Is there no hope for a reconciliation?

STEPHEN: None. Truth is we're both happier to be free.

JOE: I'm not in that position.

STEPHEN: I realize that, which leads me to the second reason for my call. *(He looks around again.)* But let's first at least order our drinks. Waitress!

JOE: *(Laughing)* There won't be any waitress.

STEPHEN: No waitress? What kind of place is this?

JOE: I was surprised you chose it.

STEPHEN: Actually, I've never been here before. It looked quiet.

JOE: Oh, it's that. Second reason?

STEPHEN: Yes. Well. You know I'm teaching now? Here at the university?

JOE: I hadn't heard, no.

STEPHEN: Fabulous gig. I mean one is given the opportunity to open the minds of your students, nurture your students, mentor your students—

JOE: Sleep with your students.

STEPHEN: Sleep with your students, right. Not so bad.

JOE: *(Wryly)* I can see you're in heaven.

STEPHEN: The real-life equivalent, yes. Why not join me? Together we'd have even more fun.

JOE: Teach? Me?

STEPHEN: Yes! Say a chair in the business school? They'd do back flips to get you.

JOE: Stephen, thank you, but I'm perfectly happy in my job.

STEPHEN: Are you?

JOE: As I said—

STEPHEN: Are you, Joe? Are you really? Because I heard you lost your job.

*(Beat)*

JOE: I'm still trading in currencies.

STEPHEN: Day trading?

JOE: Yes.

STEPHEN: And how's that going for you?

JOE: I'm a bit behind.

STEPHEN: A bit?

JOE: I'm distracted.

STEPHEN: Yes.

JOE: I want Cleo back.

STEPHEN: Yes, I can see that. Have you tried to get her back?

JOE: *(Bitter laugh)* Have I tried! Only everything.

STEPHEN: So you need something, Joe—as I've been saying—to fill up the emptiness.

JOE: What about yours?

STEPHEN: I've told you.

JOE: Dangling four or five co-eds at the same time?

STEPHEN: I've actually done three. Four or five is aspirational. *(He gets up, peers around once more.)* What we really need now is our drinks! *(He starts calling in a loud voice:)* Waitress!

JOE: I promise you. If there's anything aspirational in this place, it's ever finding a waitress.

STEPHEN: It's a functioning restaurant. There are menus on the table! *(Sitting, opens his and flips pages. Stunned)* It's blank.

*(JOE nods.)*

STEPHEN: *(Spooked)* This place is telling us something.

JOE: *(Laughing)* Yeah, to get out of here. *(He gets to his feet.)*

STEPHEN: Where you going?

JOE: To plant myself on Cleo's doorstep and try again.

*(JOE makes to leave, but halts as STEPHEN starts talking.)*

STEPHEN: You know what, Joe. I have a prophesy for you. Cleo will take you back. She will be happy, because from now on you'll be good. Your boy will be very happy—then leave you for school and his own life. And you will be happy—until you're not—a condition that arrives early and stays late.

JOE: That's a dark prophesy.

STEPHEN: It's the way it happens, Joe. So join me! I have the remedy.

JOE: Sorry, Stephen. I have a different plan.

STEPHEN: Oh, yes? What?

JOE: Couldn't be simpler or better. I will be there for Cleo whenever she wants me—to lighten every one of her days.

*(Fade to black)*

### END OF ACT TWO

# ACT THREE

## Scene 1

*(Ten years later)*

*(CLEO and JOE are in bed, on top of the covers. He, dressed in pajamas, is propped up against the back board, working on his laptop. She, in a nightgown and bathrobe, sits on the front edge of the bed.)*

*(The chandelier, having moved down further, hovers above.)*

CLEO: Empty nest.

JOE: Not really. There'll be school vacations. Harry will be back for those. For a while yet.

CLEO: It's started, Joe.

JOE: Has it?

CLEO: We're getting old.

JOE: At forty?

CLEO: I'm not forty!

JOE: Not quite.

CLEO: I have *days* before I'm forty!

JOE: Shall we celebrate the event?

CLEO: With a dirge?

JOE: I thought a party.

CLEO: Three hundred of our closest friends?

JOE: I thought a more intimate number.

CLEO: Intimate. Why not! Let's have Stephen and Dorothy.

*(Silence)*

JOE: They're not a couple anymore.

CLEO: True.

JOE: And we don't see them. Either of them.

CLEO: *I* don't.

JOE: Nor I.

CLEO: That cow! *(Beat)* What happened broke up their marriage.

JOE: Not ours, thank God.

CLEO: Thank who?

JOE: *(Scampering to join* CLEO *at the edge)* Thank *you*, darling! You were wonderfully forgiving. After—

CLEO: Ten months of hell.

JOE: For both of us, yes.

*(Noise downstairs.)*

CLEO: What was that?

JOE: What?

*(Same sound)*

CLEO: *(Hoarse whisper)* That!

*(Beat)*

JOE: House creaking?

CLEO: You think?

JOE: *(Unsure)* Absolutely.

*(Bigger noise , and continuing footsteps.)*

CLEO: Someone's in this house!

JOE: I locked up! Activated the alarm!

(*Approaching footsteps*)

(*Enter* CHALMERS, *the burglar [same actor who played* STEPHEN *and* DR MALONE*], dressed in black pants and polo shirt.*)

(JOE, *screaming, leaps out of bed;* CLEO, *shrieking, leaps up to* JOE's *side as she tightens the sash to her bathrobe.*)

(CHALMERS *turns on the light.*)

CHALMERS: Very satisfying response.

JOE: Who the fuck are you?!

CHALMERS: You need this explained to you?

(JOE *rips a lamp from its socket and approaches threateningly.* CHALMERS *pulls out a hand gun.* JOE *stops in his tracks.*)

JOE: You have a gun!

CHALMERS: Brilliant!

CLEO: Get out of my house!

CHALMERS: Do you really believe I'd have gone to the trouble of invading your house only to leave at your whim?

JOE: Whim?!

CLEO: The cops are on their way!

CHALMERS: Alerted, you're thinking, by the alarm system I disengaged on my way in.

(CLEO *and* JOE *exchange looks.*)

CHALMERS: Now. First things first. Put the lamp down, Joe.

JOE: You know my name?

CHALMERS: Of course I know your name.

JOE: So this isn't chance, your breaking in here.

CHALMERS: Sort of chance. I had to start somewhere on the street. And once I picked your house—more or less at random—naturally, I did my research.

CLEO: Get out!

(CLEO *throws a slipper at* CHALMERS, *which bounces harmlessly off his chest. He looks at it with amusement.*)

CHALMERS: Okay. Let's take a moment. Cool appraisal. Where matters stand. I have a gun. You don't. I know I will use the gun, if I have to. You can't be sure. So. Risk assessment. What you have to weigh are the chances of the gun going off, if you don't do what I ask, against the downside, if any, of doing it.

CLEO: We don't *know* what you want.

CHALMERS: Precisely. So leaping at me with that lamp would be a bit premature, wouldn't you say? You should at least find out.

(JOE *sits on the bed, lamp in his lap.*)

CHALMERS: The hard core home invader would demand that the female victim tie up the male victim, then force him to watch—or, maybe worse, imagine—some unspeakable acts being perpetrated on the body of the female.

JOE: You bastard!

CHALMERS: Easy, man. Not my thing. I simply wanted you to know how much worse this could be with the wrong sort of fellow breaking in here. My interest is financial.

JOE: Take what you want.

CHALMERS: (*Ridiculing the offer*) Anything I can find?

CLEO: Just take it all and leave.

(CHALMERS *gives a big laugh.*)

CHALMERS: You have a safe?

JOE: I don't.

CHALMERS: *(Deprecatingly)* So you're offering what? The petty cash in your wallet? Maybe some loose coins?

JOE: There are paintings.

CHALMERS: *(Even more disparagingly)* I've seen the paintings.

CLEO: You're an art critic?!

CHALMERS: I know the market.

JOE: What then?

CHALMERS: You're a rich man, Joe.

JOE: You've had me investigated?

CHALMERS: There you go again. Have you never heard of the internet?

JOE: It often exaggerates.

CHALMERS: Not in your case.

JOE: There are limits!

CHALMERS: To what you'll pay for your life? Your wife's well-being?

CLEO: Joe, this is a bluff!

CHALMERS: *(With chilling menace)* You need only to call it, my dear.

CLEO: Hit him with the lamp!

JOE: I'm thinking about it.

CHALMERS: You'll throw your back out.

JOE: I'm in shape!

*(CHALMERS laughs.)*

CHALMERS: Be reasonable, Joe. I'm prepared to be.

JOE: How…reasonable?

CHALMERS: Even mil. Wire transfer.

JOE: Dollars?

CHALMERS: Pounds sterling I'd thought.

JOE: Out of the question.

CHALMERS: Don't be ridiculous. You value being alive at considerably more than that figure.

JOE: I think you *are* bluffing.

CHALMERS: Don't push me.

(JOE *smiles.*)

CHALMERS: I'd start by shooting you in the foot.

JOE: I doubt it.

CHALMERS: You're wrong to doubt.

JOE: Then shoot!

CHALMERS: Your foot's not worth a million pounds?

JOE: I never moved from dollars.

CHALMERS: Dollars then.

JOE: Why don't you just take the paintings and leave?

CHALMERS: I'll shoot your wife.

CLEO: Bullshit.

CHALMERS: You think I won't?

(CLEO *picks up the phone;* CHALMERS *shoots one of the paintings off the wall. She puts down the phone, now terrified.*)

(*Silence*)

CHALMERS: Shall we get back to the wire transfer?

(JOE *stands.*)

JOE: I'm giving you nothing.

CHALMERS: You're welshing on the million?!

JOE: I never agreed to it.

CHALMERS: As good as!

JOE: That's *your* version.

CHALMERS: Then you leave me no choice.

JOE: You've lots of choices. Walking out the door, for example.

CHALMERS: Empty-handed? You must be joking. Tell you what, though. I'll give you a chance. Turn it into a game.

(CHALMERS *opens the gun chamber and removes four bullets, spins it and shows the one loaded chamber to both* CLEO *and* JOE. *He then spins it again and closes it without looking.*)

CHALMERS: I'm leaving in the one bullet.

(CHALMERS *again points the gun at* JOE.)

JOE: You wouldn't!

CHALMERS: Oh, but I would, and will. You start with one in six odds. They keep going down, of course.

JOE: You could keep re-spinning it.

CHALMERS: (*Getting into the wonderful math of it all*) Hmm. The odds on each spin would be one in six. But, on the average, if one were to keep playing, the gun would go off every three to four pulls of the trigger. Curious anomaly.

JOE: (*Joining in*) More interesting then to re-spin it. Of course, I don't think the basic odds are one in six.

CHALMERS: How could they be otherwise?

JOE: You're ignoring the effect of gravity, which will tend to pull the one bullet toward six o'clock.

CLEO: Joe!

CHALMERS: You are taking this rather cooly.

JOE: Am I?

CHALMERS: You realize—in two minutes you may be dead.

JOE: Yes.

CHALMERS: We're talking only money here.

JOE: Are we?

CHALMERS: You wouldn't even miss a million dollars.

CLEO: Give him the money, Joe.

JOE: I don't think so.

CHALMERS: You want to die?!

JOE: Of course not. But I'm curious about it. Who isn't?

CHALMERS: Am I hearing this right? Or is this simply a ploy?

JOE: Let's play the game. Say three times. If I'm still alive, you leave.

CLEO: *I'll* give you the money!

JOE: She doesn't have it.

CLEO: What are you doing, Joe?

(CHALMERS *aims the gun at* JOE's *head.*)

CHALMERS: Say goodbye, Joe.

JOE: Ha!

(CHALMERS *pulls the trigger and we hear a click.*)

CLEO: Joe, please! It's not funny!

JOE: Again!

CLEO: No!

(CLEO *makes a move at* CHALMERS, *who stops her with a wave of the gun.*)

CHALMERS: Oy! (*Re-pointing at* JOE, *he squeezes the trigger; another click.*) Odds now one in three.

JOE: I'll take them.

CHALMERS: You're crazy!

JOE: No doubt.

CHALMERS: *(Waving the gun at* JOE*)* This is the one, I think. With your death written all over it.

JOE: Pull the fucking trigger, man!

CLEO: *Don't!*

CHALMERS: Oh, what the hell.

*(Loud gunshot. Ululations from* JOE. *Shrieks from* CLEO. *But he's alive.)*

CLEO: Joe!

*(*JOE *puts his hand to his face.)*

CHALMERS: You got balls, Joe.

*(*JOE*'s still not sure he's survived.)*

CHALMERS: How'd you know? One real bullet, the rest blanks—fools everyone.

JOE: I didn't. Know.

CHALMERS: Come on! What was my tell?

JOE: No tell.

*(*CHALMERS *looks at* JOE *inquiringly.)*

CHALMERS: Random choice? To die, not die, same thing?

JOE: *(Sitting on the bed)* I *know* the difference.

CHALMERS: Just *makes* no difference?

JOE: What's your name?

CHALMERS: Why on earth would I give you my name?

*(*JOE *shrugs.)*

JOE: I'll call you…Chalmers.

CHALMERS: Chalmers?

JOE: You look like a Chalmers.

CHALMERS: You're actually enjoying this!

(JOE *shrugs;* CHALMERS *ponders the matter some more.*)

CHALMERS: Yes. I get it.

CLEO: You do?

CHALMERS: Of course I do. This experience—living the possibility of immediate extinction—quite revivifying, wasn't it? Enriching, I should think.

JOE: Had its moments.

CHALMERS: So how shall we settle the matter?

JOE: Settle what?!

CHALMERS: My bill. For services rendered.
Call it two hundred thousand? Euros.

JOE: You expect to be paid?

CHALMERS: For enriching your experience? I should certainly hope so! A small deposit in my account. (*She picks up her cell phone, dials three digits.*) How's this, whatever your name is? We get the cops here in five minutes to deposit *you* behind bars.

CHALMERS: No need for that.

CLEO: (*To the 911 operator*) Hold a moment please. (*She looks at* CHALMERS.) You'll be going then?

CHALMERS: I'll just take a painting.

CLEO: No, you won't!

He pouts.

CLEO: (*Speaking into the receiver*) Yes, we're at 18 Marigold Lane, and there's a burglar in our home. Right now. Could you— Yes, thank you. (*She gives* CHALMERS *a hard stare.*)

CHALMERS: Toodaloo.

*(CHALMER exits.* CLEO *shuts the phone.)*

*(Long silence)*

JOE: *(Sardonically)* I didn't see that happening.

CLEO: *(Some ire)* It didn't *just* happen, Joe.

JOE: No. *(Beat)* It didn't just.

CLEO: You contributed!

JOE: To frightening you, sorry.

CLEO: *(Getting upset)* You need thrills?

JOE: Doesn't everyone?

CLEO: Not like that!

JOE: Plugs the holes.

CLEO: What holes?

JOE: The little cavities, the tiny fissures, the lacunae.

CLEO: You scared me, Joe.

JOE: We all have them.

*(Silence)*

CLEO: Shit, I have them too.

JOE: The lacunae?

CLEO: Yes.

JOE: Because of what I said.

CLEO: No.

JOE: Because of that man, Chalmers?

CLEO: No. I think…because Harry's gone.

JOE: Meaning they've always been there. And Harry covered them up, but I can't.

CLEO: What do we do?

JOE: What we always do.

CLEO: Make the best of it.

JOE: Yes! That's what we do! Make the best of it!

CLEO: *(Attempt at rousing enthusiasm)* Because the best is not so bad!

JOE: Not bad at all.

*(Beat)*

CLEO: Among so many horrors.

JOE: Like people invading your home.

CLEO: *(More emphatically)* Like killing fields! Holocausts! Genocide!

JOE: Like existing as we do. Concocting our reality.

*(Beat)*

CLEO: Where'd that come from?

JOE: Seemed to fit.

CLEO: You're rambling again.

JOE: Yes.

CLEO: Dithering!

JOE: I...seem to do that.

CLEO: *(Despairingly, as if recognizing it for the first time)* Me too! *(Beat)* Well, let's just put a stop to it, shall we?

JOE: Sooner the better.

CLEO: Can you? Stop?

JOE: *(Breezily)* Any time.

CLEO: Like...right now?

JOE: Absolutely.

CLEO: Done.

*(Silence)*

JOE: That's no help at all!

CLEO: *(Slightly desperately)* Nope!

*(Lights out.)*

## Scene 2

*(Summer house, ten years later, evening.)*

*(CLEO and JOE are reading in the living room of their summer house in Rhode Island. French doors at the end of the room offer a view of the bay. A storm rattles the windows.)*

*(And now the chandelier seems a bit lower than a chandelier should be.)*

*(Clanging sound)*

CLEO: That buoy…sounds louder than usual.

JOE: That would be the storm.

CLEO: What storm?

JOE: They're talking about hundred mile an hour winds.

CLEO: They always exaggerate.

JOE: True.

*(CLEO gives JOE a quizzical look, to which he merely shrugs, and they go back to reading.)*

CLEO: This old house…

JOE: What about it?

CLEO: Damn good thing!

JOE: *(As if obvious)* Ye-ah!.

CLEO: Paid nothing for it.

JOE: Well, as for that ….

CLEO: What?

JOE: It's falling apart, darling. Costs a fortune to keep up.

CLEO: Like us.

JOE: What?

CLEO: We're falling apart too.

(JOE *sits up abruptly.*)

JOE: We are not!

CLEO: I am. Over fifty. And I hate to think what's going on in you, given *your* age.

JOE: I'm totally fit!

CLEO: Ha!

JOE: *(With umbrage)* Do I *look* different?

CLEO: From when? Twenty-five years ago? What do you think?!

JOE: *(Confidence waning)* Better or worse?

CLEO: Try to be serious, Joe.

JOE: I'm perfectly serious.

CLEO: One has tires on one's midriff.

JOE: Whose midriff?!

CLEO: Yours! Mine! And look at your hair!

(JOE*'s hands go to his hair, his face a gaping question.*)

CLEO: It's thin.

JOE: Who likes fat hair?

CLEO: Joke all you want.

JOE: Why not? Why not just laugh at it?

CLEO: Because it's not funny, Joe! We are getting old. We are less than we were. We will shrivel. We will die.

JOE: We have time for lunch?

*(Doorbell)*

(CLEO *and* JOE *look at each other.*)

CLEO: Are we home?

JOE: No.

CLEO: It might be Harry.

JOE: Without calling ahead? No way. Not our Harry.

CLEO: He's perfect, isn't he?

JOE: In every way.

CLEO: Except one.

JOE: His not visiting us.

CLEO: *(Aroused)* I'd say that detracts from his perfection big time!

*(Doorbell, more insistently.)*

JOE: I'll go.

*(Enter ALBERTA [before JOE can get to the door], their spinster neighbor, a woman twenty years older than CLEO [played by the same actor who played DOROTHY, et al].)*

ALBERTA: Door's unlocked.

JOE: Alberta! Come in! How good to see you.

ALBERTA: *(Advancing into the room)* You won't be saying that in a minute.

JOE: Oh?

CLEO: *(Standing)* Hi, Alberta.

JOE: We're in the middle of a ghastly conversation which you can only relieve.

*(ALBERTA pulls off her slicker, which JOE hangs up, and sits on the edge of the sofa. CLEO takes the seat next to her.)*

ALBERTA: Doubt it. Given *my* news.

JOE: Before dispatching your news, what to drink?

ALBERTA: Nothing, thank you. Dispatch and be off, that's me. If you haven't heard, they're evacuating the area.

CLEO: Oh, Christ!

JOE: *(Making light of it)* Because of a hurricane in South Carolina?

ALBERTA: It *is* heading toward us.

JOE: They always do. Then peter out on Cape May.

CLEO: *(Musing)* Never been to Cape May. Have you? Where the hurricanes go to die.

ALBERTA: The authorities—

JOE: Over-react. Always.

ALBERTA: Not in '38, they didn't.

JOE: And that was how many years ago?

ALBERTA: *I* remember it. Took most of the houses down around here. My sister and me—we were floating in that bay on a mattress!

CLEO: I've heard such stories, yes.

ALBERTA: I'm a warden now.

CLEO: I know.

ALBERTA: It's my job to tell everyone.

JOE: Of course it is.

ALBERTA: What they do with the information is up to them.

JOE: Yes. And in our case—

ALBERTA: You'll wait it out.

CLEO: We will!

ALBERTA: You're on the water here, exposed.

JOE: We'll be fine.

ALBERTA: You can bunk at my place, if you want. It's on higher ground.

CLEO: So you're leaving?

ALBERTA: No. I'll be there too. In my case, no reason not to. Be a blessing, actually, if it came to that. Floating away again on a mattress. I wouldn't like the drowning part. But I'm ready for it. I have the drugs.

*(Beat)*

CLEO: What on earth are you talking about?

ALBERTA: You don't want to know.

CLEO: As if we still had that option, Alberta!

*(ALBERTA laughs.)*

JOE: *(Carefully)* You said drugs....

ALBERTA: They give you morphine. Lovely stuff!

JOE: They?

ALBERTA: *(Defensively)* It's prescribed.

JOE: I see. *(He sits on a side chair.)*

ALBERTA: Yes.

JOE: Taken a bit already, have you?

ALBERTA: Oh, yeah!

CLEO: *(Hushed tones)* You have cancer, Alberta?

ALBERTA: So there it is.

JOE: But you're being treated.

ALBERTA: That's the thing. You're given the choice: you can be poisoned by all the wonderful drugs they've come up with—after a hundred billion dollars of research—or let the big dog eat, as we say in the radiology pavilion.

CLEO: I can understand why you're angry.

ALBERTA: *(Furious)* Angry?!

*(They sit there looking at each other.)*

*(ALBERTA gets up, they also rise.)*

ALBERTA: No graceful way to end this, is there?

*(Silence)*

ALBERTA: It's in my liver, and it's spreading. You know what that means? *(She starts putting on her slicker.)* Best case? I've got days, no more. So I'm not really frightened of the hurricane.

JOE: Isn't there anything—

ALBERTA: One can do? *(She looks at them with amused pity.)*

CLEO: *(Low voice)* What *are* you frightened of?

ALBERTA: Good. We're going to talk about that, are we?

CLEO: *(Trepidatiously)* If you like.

*(*ALBERTA *sits again; they follow.)*

ALBERTA: Of course I like. That's what I've got. I'm looking at horror. I frighten you, you sympathize with me. It's a kick. I've no idea why.

JOE: We're all scared of dying.

ALBERTA: Not like this, you're not. Years away, you're easy, comfortable, philosophical. Wait 'till it's in your face. When you're lookin' at: lights out, baby! All gone, no more you, boom!

CLEO: I don't know what to say.

ALBERTA: In this, I do the saying! You do the platitudes.

*(Beat)*

JOE: *(Kindly, but disingenuously)* There's a point, Alberta. We just don't know what it is. Maybe you're about to find out.

ALBERTA: You really believe that?

*(*JOE *shrugs.)*

ALBERTA: If there were a point, we'd all know it by now.

JOE: Most people think they do.

ALBERTA: Frankly…I just want to get on with it.

CLEO: You're thinking—maybe after all—there's something to get on to?

ALBERTA: *(Sarcastically)* You bet.

CLEO: We wouldn't know, then, would we? So we wouldn't care. About there being no point.

ALBERTA: Oh, I'd care. Some form of me would care.

CLEO: So you do believe!

ALBERTA: I don't really know what I'm saying.

CLEO: You're just rambling a bit.

ALBERTA: Blithering is what I'm doing. Blithering in the face of death. Wait till it's your turn. You'll see!

*(ALBERTA gets up again, forcing CLEO and JOE to follow.)*

ALBERTA: So? More platitudes?

*(CLEO and JOE stammer in confusion and shake their heads.)*

ALBERTA: *(Leaving)* See ya! Maybe. Maybe not. *(She exits.)*

CLEO: Wow.

JOE: Yeah.

*(CLEO sits.)*

CLEO: I *didn't* know what to say. Really.

*(JOE sits.)*

JOE: There's nothing ever to say.

CLEO: There must be something.

JOE: To say?

CLEO: To do.

JOE: By us?

CLEO: Yes, by us. I know! We could take a trip.

JOE: Right now?

CLEO: Of course not right now. But we can talk about it right now. Plan it.

JOE: All right. Where would you like to go?

CLEO: Someplace that doesn't have hurricanes.

JOE: Everyplace has something.

CLEO: Something bad.

JOE: With the good.

CLEO: *(Anguished)* Alberta—she may die...in *days,* she said!

JOE: Let's not think about it.

CLEO: *(Sarcastically)* Oh, that works!

JOE: Nothing...works!

*(Silence)*

CLEO: So where would *you* like to go?

*(JOE thinks about that.)*

JOE: Somewhere adventurous...and romantic...like, say, Pamplona.

CLEO: Getting gored by bulls?

JOE: How 'bout Venice?

CLEO: Great idea.

JOE: We've never been.

CLEO: Never!

JOE: So that's the plan.

CLEO: Venice! *(Beat)* Which is a crumbling city.

JOE: All the more reason to see it. Now.

CLEO: Before *we* crumble.

*(JOE makes a pained expression.)*

JOE: *(Emphatically)* There really isn't any need, darling, to put the morbid spin on it.

CLEO: *(With sudden false cheer)* Or need to whistle Dixie!

JOE: But that's what we do, you're saying?

CLEO: It's our alternative to dithering.

*(CLEO and JOE spring up and flash smiles.)*

*(Loud band rendition of first few bars of the song, Dixie, to which CLEO and JOE, in a burst of frenzied energy, dance and whistle.)*

*(They stop abruptly.)*

*(Silence)*

JOE: That doesn't help either.

CLEO: Of course it doesn't. And it's a racist song, besides.

JOE: Lincoln loved it.

CLEO: Got him shot. Almost got you shot. Remember?!

*(Silence)*

JOE: Can we talk about something else?

*(Lights fade, and back up, to:)*


## Scene 3

*(Small art museum in Venice)*

*(Enter ARTURO, a handsome middle-aged guide [same actor who played CHALMERS, et al], leading CLEO and JOE into a well-lit white-washed room, with a wooden bench in front of a single large painting.)*

*(The chandelier now just hovers above their heads.)*

ARTURO: Signor, Signora—*this*, above all, I wanted you to see!

*(The painting is of a prepubescent girl, standing nude in profile, admiring her self in a looking glass.)*

JOE: *(Amused)* Someone painting in the style of Balthus?

ARTURO: Indeed. Someone named... *(With a flourish)* ... Balthasar Klossowski.

JOE: You're saying, Balthus himself painted this?

*(ARTURO nods.)*

*(JOE goes closer, studies the painting. CLEO stands off.)*

JOE: I don't think so.

ARTURO: Why should you doubt it?

JOE: For one thing, the painting looks recent. Balthus died years ago. For another... *(He gives the painting another look.)* Wait. Is this a finished work?

ARTURO: Aha! You see, you see! You've seen through to the problem. Not finished. Which may give it the *appearance* of something done recently. But still magnificent, don't you think? It was found last year.

JOE: In Venice? Balthus lived in Rome.

ARTURO: Correct. It was found in Roma and brought to Venezia. You seem to know a good deal about Balthus.

CLEO: Oh, Joe's a big fan. Pictures of prepubescents? Naked?

ARTURO: *(Musically)* To each his own.

JOE: *(Annoyed)* As it happens, I'm not drawn to such subjects. What about you?

ARTURO: I prefer art that celebrates...more mature women. *(He glances at CLEO and smiles.)*

JOE: *(Mounting irritation)* In their fifties, for example?

ARTURO: Especially when they look so much younger. *(He bows.)* I will give you time alone...with this painting. It's quite… *(Through his teeth)* authentic. *(He exits.)*

JOE: What was that all about?

CLEO: He's just trying to be gallant.

JOE: *(Half-joking)* By making a pass at my wife?

CLEO: A pass? More like a follow-through.

JOE: *(Serious)* He's already made a pass?

CLEO: When you were in the Gents. What he *said* was, "Will you have dinner with me tonight?"

JOE: *(Flabbergasted)* He's asking you to dinner?!

CLEO: He's asking me to bed, Joe. "Dinner" is what he's calling it.

JOE: That's outrageous!

CLEO: Depends on your point of view.

JOE: There can be two points of view on this?!

CLEO: Which is why I told you. So you could help me decide whether to accept.

*(*JOE* sits hard on the bench.)*

JOE: I see. This is retribution. For something done twenty years ago.

CLEO: No, Joe, think. As I did. Twenty years ago I had—at first—the conventional reaction. Then I realized, for you it was one crazy night. Probably made you feel great. Cost me, ultimately, nothing.

JOE: *(Trying to come to grips with the facts)* So now you want to have sex with a sleazy tour guide.

CLEO: Handsome tour guide. And it's always been a fantasy of mine. It'll take ten minutes.

JOE: To destroy our lives!

CLEO: My life wasn't destroyed twenty years ago.

JOE: You're more flexible than me.

CLEO: So I lose out because you're less flexible?

JOE: Why are you telling me about this…this debauchery you're planning?

CLEO: To give you a vote.

JOE: Really? And how do you think I might cast it? The fact you want to have sex with another person is devastating.

CLEO: *You* wanted to.

JOE: I didn't, actually. It was thrust upon me, as it were.

CLEO: You didn't resist.

JOE: I resisted a little bit.

CLEO: You didn't even tell me about it. Voluntarily. I had to worm it out of you.

JOE: You think announcing it beforehand makes it better?

CLEO: Makes it above board.

JOE: Makes it premeditated!

CLEO: What exactly makes *you* so upset about this?

JOE: You're kidding!

CLEO: No. Seriously. Try to tell me in terms that aren't conclusory. Is it sheer possessiveness?

JOE: No!

CLEO: Some weird religious angle?

JOE: Of course not.

CLEO: It can't be that you believe there's some spiritual good in being utterly faithful. You weren't.

*(Beat)*

JOE: *I'm* a hypocrite.

CLEO: Meaning you believe in faithfulness for me, but not necessarily for you.

JOE: It's different for the man. As an anthropologist, you know that.

CLEO: For some women vis-a-vis some men, it's different. Maybe. But not for me. If you can, I can.

JOE: For ten minutes, you're saying—ten shabby minutes—and then expect everything between us to be as it was?

CLEO: Not entirely, no. And it's the sex part that would likely take ten minutes. The whole...business...would take the night.

JOE: You'd have to take your clothes off.

CLEO: I expect he's seen whatever I have to show him.

JOE: But *you* haven't shown it. To anyone but me.

CLEO: True. But I'm feeling it's time, don't you think? Before it's all gone?

(JOE *jumps off the bench and throws out his arms.*)

JOE: This is awful!

CLEO: Get a grip, Joe.

JOE: I can't believe ! I can't imagine...!

CLEO: You can't even tell me why it is you're so against this.

JOE: You'll break our bond.

CLEO: But you've already broken it. Didn't kill us. You still love me, I know that.

JOE: (*With genuine feeling*) What I know is...if you do this, it will hurt. So much so I'm not sure I'll be able to stand it.

(*Long silence in which* CLEO *considers her response.*)

CLEO: Then I won't.

JOE: You won't?

CLEO: No. I'll tell him, no.

*(Beat)*

JOE: Have you been having me on?

CLEO: Certainly not.

*(JOE goes to CLEO.)*

JOE: The man asked you to dinner?

CLEO: As I said.

JOE: And you were seriously considering going to bed with him?

CLEO: Yes. Considering.

JOE: Depending on how I reacted?

*(CLEO takes JOE's hands.)*

CLEO: Yes.

JOE: And did anything surprise you in the way I reacted?

CLEO: How deep it is in you, yes.

JOE: What…is, exactly?

CLEO: Your need.

*(JOE looks confused.)*

JOE: *(Softly)* My *need*? For you…of course.

CLEO: Yes.

JOE: You meant something more.

*(CLEO shakes her head "no" while it's obvious she's still holding back.)*

*(ARTURO walks in.)*

ARTURO: I'm interrupting.

*(CLEO and JOE break apart.)*

JOE: We've considered your offer to my wife and decided against accepting it.

ARTURO: You've had a good long family discussion about it?

JOE: We have.

ARTURO: But perhaps now you'll want to reconsider.

JOE: *(Incredulous)* Not on your life!

ARTURO: Interesting locution, in the circumstances.

JOE: What…circumstances?

ARTURO: You haven't heard then. How could you have? *I've* just heard, and you've been cloistered in here. About the water surge. In less than two hours. Few are likely to survive it. There simply aren't enough boats.

CLEO: Water surge?

ARTURO: A rise of ten, fifteen meters is predicted. Venezia is as good as gone. That's always been a risk, but it will be strange, now, to see it actually happen.

*(ARTURO observes CLEO and JOE's stupefaction.)*

ARTURO: *(Cheerfully)* Well, have to be off.

JOE: We'll be right with you.

ARTURO: No, no. Boat's not large enough for you.

CLEO: We came in the boat.

ARTURO: That was before.

JOE: Before what?

ARTURO: Don't be naive.

JOE: We hired your boat for the day!

ARTURO: In a different world. That was the world of everything as it should be. This is the world of the surge. Which has arrived a little more rapidly than expected.

CLEO: You can't possibly just abandon us!

(ARTURO *shrugs.*)

JOE: I'll have you before the authorities!

ARTURO: *(Laughing)* The authorities? My dear Meester Allworthy. These islands are sinking and the authorities along with them. They have more immediate concerns than your claim for unrendered services. Like finding boats for themselves. Like their not drowning. So, if you will excuse me....

JOE: You can't have my wife.

ARTURO: Yes, I understood you had made that choice.

JOE: And if we hadn't?

(ARTURO *shrugs.*)

JOE: Those are your terms?! My wife or my life?!

ARTURO: Not exactly. *Your* life doesn't really enter into it.

CLEO: You'll save me, but not him?

ARTURO: I too must make choices.

CLEO: *(Dramatically)* As do I. You take both of us or neither.

ARTURO: I'm not into three-ways.

CLEO: Nor are we.

ARTURO: Ciao!

CLEO: *(Momentarily rethinking)* Not so fast.

(ARTURO *looks from* JOE *to* CLEO *and back again.*)

(JOE *reflects.*)

JOE: You go with him. I'll find another boat.

CLEO: No!

JOE: I insist.

CLEO: I'm staying with you.

(ARTURO *laughs uproariously.*)

ARTURO: *(English accent)* Well done! The both of you!

JOE: You're not Italian.

ARTURO: Goodness, no.

JOE: You're English!

ARTURO: *(American accent)* Sorry. Not English.

JOE: What the hell kind of game are you playing here?

ARTURO: *(German accent)* Verdammt! Just a game.
There's no surge, at least for now. So it's like the game
of the city itself. Venedig, seemingly immutable and
resplendent, is, underneath, a tarnished hag, ready to
die. But no, just for today, the illusion continues.

JOE: In other words, you made it all up.

ARTURO: Rather inventive, don't you think?

JOE: To get my wife into bed?

ARTURO: That would have been an ancillary benefit.

JOE: For what other conceivable purpose?

ARTURO: *(American accent)* Sheer whimsey. I find life
otherwise very dull.

CLEO: And the Balthus?

ARTURO: *(Laughing)* Balthus?! You believed that too?!

JOE: You scoundrel!

ARTURO: Yes. But I do have news.

CLEO: Why would we believe anything you say?

ARTURO: There's always the possibility I'm telling the
truth.

CLEO: And in this case?

ARTURO: *(Bored now)* Easy enough to confirm. There's another hurricane brewing in the Caribbean. Looks like the worst ever. Landfall likely in several days. The place already predicted.

*(CLEO and JOE gape at him.)*

ARTURO: Did you say you had a house on the southern tip of Rhode Island?

*(CLEO and JOE continue to gape.)*

ARTURO: That's the spot.

*(Lights out)*

## Scene 4

*(Lights up, but dim.)*

*(Night)*

*(CLEO, in a nightgown, stands swaying on the chandelier— now a buoy. Next to her, JOE, in pajamas, sleeps with his arm looped around the mast of the buoy. They gently rock back and forth.)*

*(Lighting effects create the illusion they are floating in the sea.)*

*(A cloud releases the moon, brightening the buoy.)*

*(She stirs him.)*

CLEO: Wake up, Joe!

*(JOE does.)*

CLEO: *(Desperately)* We're in what used to be the bay in front of what used to be our house.

JOE: *(Dazzedly)* It's still the bay.

CLEO: It's not. It used to be a bay because it sat in the middle of what used to be a five-mile U-shaped formation of land. But now, there is no U, there is no land; we're in the middle of the goddamn ocean! Hanging onto this…thing, this buoy. And there've been no boats. Whatta we do?

(JOE *struggles to his feet, gazes about.*)

JOE: You think we have options?

(CLEO *looks at* JOE *with horror.*)

CLEO: I'm freezing. I'm wet and I'm freezing. And starving.

JOE: It will be morning soon. The sun will be out.

CLEO: If we live until morning.

(*Beat*)

JOE: I wasn't really sleeping. I was thinking.

CLEO: With your eyes closed?

JOE: Yes. I was thinking about our life together.

CLEO: And?

JOE: I promised you ecstatic love.

CLEO: I remember.

JOE: Have you felt it?

CLEO: Every day, Joe.

JOE: Me too.

(*Silence*)

JOE: We don't talk about that.

CLEO: We don't have to.

JOE: No. We don't.

(*The buoy stops swaying.* JOE *looks out over the water.*)

JOE: Maybe I can catch a fish. Possibly a bird.

CLEO: I haven't seen any birds.

JOE: Nor I.

CLEO: Joe, we're going to die here.

JOE: Someone will come along.

CLEO: You don't know that!

JOE: No, I don't know it. Good chance, though.

CLEO: Why? The hurricane was awful. A tidal wave destroyed all the houses. Very likely it destroyed all the boats.

JOE: We're alive.

CLEO: Are we?

JOE: Of course we are.

CLEO: We're not rocking any more.

JOE: The calm after the storm.

CLEO: It's never this calm.

JOE: The bigger the storm, the bigger the calm.

CLEO: You just made that up.

JOE: Yes, but it sounds right.

CLEO: What are we going to do, Joe?

JOE: Now the possibilities may be endless.

CLEO: Oh? You see one? Other than hanging onto this stupid buoy?

JOE: If you're right about the calm, we should be able to step out onto the water and walk.

CLEO: *(With dread)* What do you mean, right about the calm?

JOE: You know. What you said.

CLEO: *(Frantic)* I didn't say anything!

JOE: Questioned then.

CLEO: Whether we're really alive?

JOE: Yes. If you're right, and we aren't, this water is a delusion. Should I try it?

CLEO: No!

JOE: Afraid to find out?

CLEO: Yes!

JOE: You don't seem cold any more.

CLEO: I may be going mad.

JOE: Two days on a buoy could do that.

CLEO: Are you enjoying this?

JOE: It's different.

CLEO: Joe.

JOE: What?

CLEO: I thought I saw something.

JOE: What?!

*(A black cloud covers the moon—*CLEO *and* JOE *are in darkness.)*

CLEO: I can't see *anything now.*

JOE: Easy, darling.

*(A voice in the darkness)*

STEPHEN: Ahoy, ahoy!

CLEO: I know that voice.

*(Another voice in the darkness:)*

DOROTHY: Is there someone on that buoy?

JOE: Oh my God!

*(The cloud lifts. Below them, staring up, are* DOROTHY *and* STEPHEN—*hanging on to the edge of the buoy.)*

JOE: You two!

STEPHEN: Can we come up?

JOE: No!

STEPHEN: No?!

JOE: There's not enough room. And what are you doing here?

STEPHEN: Looking for buoys of course.

JOE: Well, you can't have this one, and that's not what I meant. What are you doing in this part of the world, and how come you're together?

STEPHEN: Oh, we've been together for weeks. Fully reconciled. We came to tell you. Our oldest friends. Which is why we're in the neighborhood.

CLEO: Didn't you hear the warnings?

STEPHEN: Of course. But the authorities always overreact to these things.

CLEO: Well, they didn't overreact to this one!

DOROTHY: Can we come up now?

JOE: If we let you up here, four people die, instead of two go on living.

STEPHEN: Now who's overreacting? There's plenty of room.

JOE: There are plenty of buoys! One not two hundred yards from here!

(STEPHEN *starts trying to climb aboard.*)

STEPHEN: *(To* DOROTHY*)* Come on darling!

CLEO: Go for another buoy!

STEPHEN: This one's fine.

(STEPHEN *lands on the edge of the buoy, and hoists his wife up, also to a sitting position, but their struggle tips the buoy dangerously.* CLEO *and* JOE, *trying for footholds, are virtually dangling off the other end.*)

STEPHEN: See. Plenty of room.

CLEO: You'll kill us all!

STEPHEN: I don't think so. Much more cozy. Among friends.

JOE: Are you blithering?

STEPHEN: No, Joe. I'm a changed man. I see the bright side now. Of everything.

JOE: Such as four people clinging to a buoy in the middle of the Atlantic!

STEPHEN: Of everything!

CLEO: Really? I seem to recall—

STEPHEN: A different me.

CLEO: No longer fascinated with nothingness?

STEPHEN: Absolutely not. It's the here and now for me that's beautiful. Focus on that.

*(He leaps to his feet, shoving CLEO and JOE even further to the edge.)*

STEPHEN: Up you go, darling.

*(STEPHEN pulls DOROTHY up along side and looks around.)*

STEPHEN: You know, Joe, you were right about there being no room up here.

JOE: Then go back in the water. Plenty of room in there.

STEPHEN: After swimming a mile to get here? You must be crazy.

CLEO: *(Shouting)* Look! Right there! A short swim. Another buoy! Go for it!

DOROTHY: Why don't you?

CLEO: We were here first!

STEPHEN: And you think what? We're in a fucking playground?

JOE: If you don't leave now....

STEPHEN: You'll what?

(JOE *rolls his eyes.*)

STEPHEN: Always comes down to that, doesn't it? Kill or be killed.

JOE: *(Dejectedly)* You know I wouldn't. That's the problem.

*(Beat)*

DOROTHY: We could try to make it work. We've been in the water for hours. You two could go back in, hold on for a while until we got dry, then we could trade places.

JOE: *(With a pretense of innocence)* You'd let us back up when it was our turn?

STEPHEN: *(Emphatically disingenuous)* Sure.

JOE: *(To* CLEO, *falsely sweet)* Whatta you think of that plan? Getting back in the water for a few hours, trusting Stephen and Dorothy to let us back up when it's our turn to get dry?

(CLEO *looks appalled.*)

DOROTHY: I like the plan.

JOE: *(With a pretense of surprise)* Do you?

STEPHEN: So get in the water, Joe!

JOE: You bet!

(STEPHEN *throws himself at* JOE, *and the two start wrestling.*)

*(Clouds over moon—lights out.)*

*(Moon reappears.* DOROTHY *and* STEPHEN *are gone.)*

(CLEO *and* JOE *sit on the buoy perplexed.*)

JOE: What just happened?

CLEO: I don't know.

JOE: You saw them, right? Stephen and Dorothy.

CLEO: I saw something.

JOE: It was Stephen and Dorothy!

CLEO: If you say.

JOE: You're not sure of it?

CLEO: Joe, don't badger me!

JOE: I wasn't hallucinating! You saw them too!

CLEO: Then where are they?

JOE: I must have pushed them off.

(CLEO *shivers.*)

JOE: I must have.

(CLEO *turns away.*)

JOE: Could I have done that? Murdered two people?

CLEO: *(Drawing into herself)* It was only you, Joe.

JOE: There was no one there?

CLEO: We're all in the same…buoy.

JOE: So it's hopeless.

*(Silence)*

(CLEO *wraps her arms around herself. Then slowly raises her head. Then peers, as if seeing something.*)

CLEO: *(Excited)* You said a boat would come!

JOE: I didn't mean it.

CLEO: But it's true!

JOE: What?

(CLEO *points out to sea.*)

CLEO: A boat, Joe!

(JOE *looks all around frantically.*)

JOE: You see a boat?!

CLEO: Look! There!

(CLEO *turns* JOE *in the right direction.*)

JOE: Oh my God, yes! A boat! A large boat!

CLEO: Coming right toward us.

JOE: Is it real?

CLEO: Can't you see it?

JOE: Of course I see it.

CLEO: It's come to rescue us, I think.

JOE: You think?

CLEO: Why else would it be coming right at us?

JOE: It may not see us.

CLEO: So let's wave. (*She waves frantically.*) Come on Joe, wave!

(JOE *joins in.*)

CLEO: It's slowing down! Can you see? They're waving back!

JOE: I don't know.

CLEO: What?

JOE: It's a cargo ship.

CLEO: So?

JOE: I'm not sure I like this.

CLEO: What's not to like?

JOE: (*With dread*) There are all kinds of possibilities.

CLEO: Worse than dying on this buoy?

JOE: Maybe.

CLEO: What can be bad? A cargo ship!

JOE: Human cargo?

(*Silence*)

CLEO: Look, Joe! They're lowering a boat for us.

JOE: Yes.

CLEO: I think it's a good thing.

JOE: *(Weakly)* Do you?

CLEO: We were longing for a boat.

JOE: True.

CLEO: So what do you want?

JOE: *(Frayed)* Something official, maybe? Coast Guard?

CLEO: This is what's here!

JOE: Well, we have no place to run.

CLEO: Embrace it, Joe! I have a feeling about this.

JOE: Yes?

CLEO: It will turn out well.

(JOE *falls on his knees.*)

JOE: Oh, God, I hope so!

CLEO: You believe in God now?

JOE: It's an expression.

CLEO: Do you believe in the boat? The goodness of the boat?

JOE: I want to.

CLEO: Do you believe it's there?

JOE: I don't know!

CLEO: Just do, Joe! Just do!

JOE: *(Cri de coeur)* It's not that fucking simple!

(*Stage black*)

## END OF PLAY

www.ingramcontent.com/pod-product-compliance
Lightning Source LLC
Chambersburg PA
CBHW052200090426
42741CB00010B/2349